HAL•LEONARD
INSTRUMENTAL
PLAY-ALONG

AUDIO
ACCESS
INCLUDED

PLAYBACK+
Speed • Pitch • Balance • Loop

TENOR SAX

TOP HITS

T0066186

Audio arrangements by Peter Deneff

To access audio visit:
www.halleonard.com/mylibrary

Enter Code
2459-1173-1066-1541

ISBN 978-1-4950-6575-0

HAL•LEONARD®
CORPORATION
7777 W. BLUEMOUND RD. P.O. BOX 13819 MILWAUKEE, WI 53213

Visit Hal Leonard Online at
www.halleonard.com

ADVENTURE OF A LIFETIME

TENOR SAX

Words and Music by GUY BERRYMAN,
JON BUCKLAND, CHRIS MARTIN,
WILL CHAMPION, MIKKEL ERIKSEN
and TOR HERMANSEN

BUDAPEST

TENOR SAX

Words and Music by GEORGE BARNETT
and JOEL POTT

To Coda ⊕

D.S. al Coda
(no repeat)

CODA
⊕

DIE A HAPPY MAN

Tenor Sax

Words and Music by THOMAS RHETT,
JOE SPARGUR and SEAN DOUGLAS

EX'S & OH'S

TENOR SAX

Words and Music by TANNER SCHNEIDER
and DAVE BASSETT

FIGHT SONG

TENOR SAX

Words and Music by RACHEL PLATTEN
and DAVE BASSETT

HELLO

TENOR SAX

Words and Music by ADELE ADKINS
and GREG KURSTIN

To Coda ⊕   **D.S. al Coda**

mp

CODA
⊕

1.

2.

LET IT GO

TENOR SAX

Words and Music by JAMES BAY
and PAUL BARRY

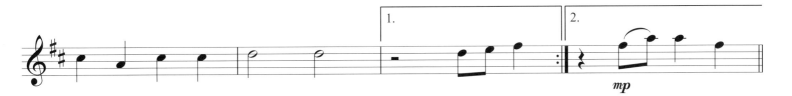

LOVE YOURSELF

TENOR SAX

Words and Music by JUSTIN BIEBER,
BENJAMIN LEVIN and ED SHEERAN

ONE CALL AWAY

TENOR SAX

Words and Music by CHARLIE PUTH,
BREYAN ISAAC, MATT PRIME,
JUSTIN FRANKS, BLAKE ANTHONY CARTER
and MAUREEN McDONALD

PILLOWTALK

TENOR SAX

Words and Music by LEVI LENNOX,
ANTHONY HANNIDES, MICHAEL HANNIDES,
ZAYN MALIK and JOE GARRETT

To Coda ⊕

D.S. al Coda
(take 3rd ending)

CODA
⊕

STITCHES

TENOR SAX

Words and Music by TEDDY GEIGER,
DANNY PARKER and DANIEL KYRIAKIDES

To Coda ⊕   **D.S. al Coda**

CODA
⊕

4

1.   2.

WRITING'S ON THE WALL

from the film SPECTRE

TENOR SAX

Words and Music by SAM SMITH
and JAMES NAPIER

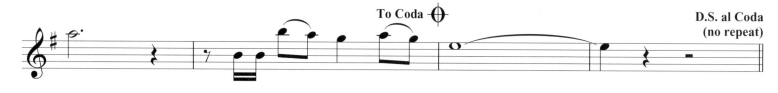